Why *Voting* Matters

Who Do People Vote For?

Kristen Rajczak Nelson

PowerKiDS press.
NEW YORK

Published in 2019 by The Rosen Publishing Group, Inc.
29 East 21st Street, New York, NY 10010

Editor: Elizabeth Krajnik
Book Design: Rachel Rising

Photo Credits: Cover, p. 17 Steve Debenport/E+/Getty Images; Cover (background), pp. 1, 3, 4 ,6, 8, 10, 12, 14, 16, 18, 20, 22, 23, 24 PepinoVerde/Shutterstock.com; p. 5 Joseph Sohm/Shutterstock.com; p. 7 Nils Versemann/Shutterstock.com; p. 9 JEFF KOWALSKY/AFP/Getty Images; p. 11 Gino Santa Maria/Shutterstock.com; p. 13 Justin Sullivan/Getty Images News/Getty Images; p. 15 Bill Clark/CQ-Roll Call Group/Getty Images; p. 19 Alex Wong/Getty Images News/Getty Images; p. 21 Matej Kastelic/Shutterstock.com; p. 22 tinbee/Shutterstock.com.

Cataloging-in-Publication Data

Names: Rajczak Nelson, Kristen.
Title: Who do people vote for? / Kristen Rajczak Nelson.
Description: New York : PowerKids Press, 2019. | Series: Why voting matters | Includes index.
Identifiers: LCCN ISBN 9781538330210 (pbk.) | ISBN 9781538330197 (library bound) | ISBN 9781538330227 (6 pack)
Subjects: LCSH: Voting--United States--Juvenile literature. | Elections--United States--Juvenile literature. | Political campaigns--United States--Juvenile literature.
Classification: LCC JK1978.R35 2019 | DDC 324.60973--dc23

Manufactured in the United States of America

CPSIA Compliance Information: Batch #CS18PK For further information contact Rosen Publishing, New York, New York at 1-800-237-9932.

Contents

By the People

In the United States, government leaders often have their jobs because people **elected** them. Before getting their position, these leaders have to make sure people know their name and face. They have to make what they stand for clear. U.S. **citizens** should do their best to learn about the people running for office!

CHANGE
WE NEED

An Official Choice

When a group of people gathers on a certain day to choose a leader, it's called an election. The **official** choice a person makes is their vote. Votes are most often cast on a piece of paper or a computer screen. In most cases, the person who gets the most votes is the winner of the election.

Who Runs?

The people trying to win an election are called candidates. There may be many candidates running for one government position. Sometimes there's only one candidate! In that case, the candidate is sure to win the election, no matter how many people vote for them.

General Election, Tuesday
Oakland County, Michigan
City of Rochester Hills, Precinct
PARTISAN SECTION
STRAIGHT PARTY TICKET
Vote for not more than 1
Republican Party
Democratic Party
Green Party
Natural Law Party
Working Class Party
STATE BOARDS
MEMBER OF THE STATE BOARD OF EDUCATION
REGENT OF THE UNIVERSITY OF MICHIGAN
Bill Weld
Darrell L. Castle
Scott N. Bradley
Jill Stein
Ajamu Baraka

On the Campaign Trail

In order to be on the **ballot** for some elections, candidates may need voters to sign a piece of paper or online **document** called a petition. Candidates speak to voters at special meetings or visit neighborhoods and meet people in their homes. Candidates often put up signs. All of this work is called campaigning.

Fighting for us
hillaryclinton.com

What They Stand For

The **political party** a candidate belongs to may be one reason voters choose a candidate. Voters also use a candidate's platform—or list of ideas about how the government should be run—to decide whether to vote for them. Candidates often make promises in their campaign about changes they'll make if they win.

IT'S TIME
TO ACT!
MEDICARE
FOR ALL!

Citizens First

There are often rules about who can run for government offices. First, all candidates in U.S. elections must be citizens, sometimes for a certain amount of time. Candidates commonly must have lived in the place where they are running for a set amount of time, too.

Age Requirement

There are also age **requirements**. These may be different from place to place. Some states allow 18-year-olds to serve in the state **legislature**. In others, candidates must be at least 25 years old. Both chambers of Congress have age requirements, too. Candidates for the Senate must be at least 30 years old.

Who Can Be President?

Candidates for president have to be born in the United States. They must be at least 35 years old. They also have to have lived within the United States for at least 14 years before running. These requirements are listed in the U.S. Constitution, which is the highest law of the United States.

Start Local

Many of the people for whom voters cast a ballot are already **politicians**. However, anyone who meets the requirements can run for a government position! Local leaders often have other jobs. They may be nurses, teachers, or parents. Many politicians start out in their local government. Some decide to run for state or federal positions.

Anyone Can Run

Even the president doesn't have to start out as a politician. President Donald Trump was a businessman first. President Lyndon Johnson was a teacher. Many presidents studied law. Most jobs have skills that can help candidates when they take office. They just have to get citizens to vote for them!

Glossary

ballot: A vote cast in an election, sometimes the piece of paper on which votes are cast.

citizen: A person who lives in a country and has the rights given to them by that country's laws.

document: A written or printed paper that gives information about something.

elect: To choose someone for a position, especially in government, by voting.

legislature: A group of people who have the power to make or change laws.

official: Recognized by the government or someone in power.

political party: A group of people with the same ideas about how the government should be run.

politician: A person who works in government, usually as an elected official.

requirement: Something that is needed before something else can be done.

Index

Websites

Due to the changing nature of Internet links, PowerKids Press has developed an online list of websites related to the subject of this book. This site is updated regularly. Please use this link to access the list: www.powerkidslinks.com/wvm/wdpvf